Melville

by Iain Gray

WRITING *to* REMEMBER

WRITING *to* REMEMBER

79 Main Street, Newtongrange,
Midlothian EH22 4NA
Tel: 0131 344 0414   Fax: 0845 075 6085
E-mail: info@lang-syne.co.uk
www.langsyneshop.co.uk

Design by Dorothy Meikle
Printed by Printwell Ltd
© Lang Syne Publishers Ltd 2021

All rights reserved. No part of this publication may be reproduced, stored or introduced into a retrieval system, or transmitted in any form or by any means (electronic, mechanical, photocopying, recording or otherwise) without the prior written permission of Lang Syne Publishers Ltd.

ISBN 978-1-85217-790-4

Melville

MOTTO:
Heaven at last

CREST:
The head of a ratchet-hound

TERRITORIES include:
Midlothian and Fife

NAME variations include:
Melvill
Melvile
Melwell
Melwill
Malwyn
Melwyn

Chapter one:

The origins of popular surnames

by George Forbes and Iain Gray

***If you don't know where you came from, you won't know where you're going* is a frequently quoted observation and one that has a particular resonance today when there has been a marked upsurge in interest in genealogy, with increasing numbers of people curious to trace their family roots.**

Main sources for genealogical research include census returns and official records of births, marriages and deaths – and the key to unlocking the detail they contain is obviously a family surname, one that has been 'inherited' and passed from generation to generation.

No matter our station in life, we all have a surname – but it was not until about the middle of the fourteenth century that the practice of being identified by a particular surname became commonly established throughout the British Isles.

Previous to this, it was normal for a person to be identified through the use of only a forename.

But as population gradually increased and there were many more people with the same forename, surnames were adopted to distinguish one person, or community, from another.

Many common English surnames are patronymic in origin, meaning they stem from the forename of one's father – with 'Johnson,' for example, indicating 'son of John.'

It was the Normans, in the wake of their eleventh century conquest of Anglo-Saxon England, a pivotal moment in the nation's history, who first brought surnames into usage – although it was a gradual process.

For the Normans, these were names initially based on the title of their estates, local villages and chateaux in France to distinguish and identify these landholdings.

Such grand descriptions also helped enhance the prestige of these warlords and generally glorify their lofty positions high above the humble serfs slaving away below in the pecking order who had only single names, often with Biblical connotations as in Pierre and Jacques.

The only descriptive distinctions among the peasantry concerned their occupations, like 'Pierre the swineherd' or 'Jacques the ferryman.'

Roots of surnames that came into usage in England not only included Norman-French, but also Old French, Old Norse, Old English, Middle English, German, Latin, Greek, Hebrew and the Gaelic languages of the Celts.

The Normans themselves were originally Vikings, or 'Northmen', who raided, colonised and eventually settled down around the French coastline.

They had sailed up the Seine in their longboats in 900AD under their ferocious leader Rollo and ruled the roost in north eastern France before sailing over to conquer England in 1066 under Duke William of Normandy – better known to posterity as William the Conqueror, or King William I of England.

Granted lands in the newly-conquered England, some of their descendants later acquired territories in Wales, Scotland and Ireland – taking not only their own surnames, but also the practice of adopting a surname, with them.

But it was in England where Norman rule and custom first impacted, particularly in relation to the adoption of surnames.

This is reflected in the famous *Domesday Book*, a massive survey of much of England and Wales, ordered by William I, to determine who owned what, what it was worth and therefore how much they were liable to pay in taxes to the voracious Royal Exchequer.

Completed in 1086 and now held in the National Archives in Kew, London, 'Domesday' was an Old English word meaning 'Day of Judgement.'

This was because, in the words of one contemporary chronicler, "its decisions, like those of the Last Judgement, are unalterable."

It had been a requirement of all those English landholders – from the richest to the poorest – that they identify themselves for the purposes of the survey and for future reference by means of a surname.

This is why the *Domesday Book*, although written in Latin as was the practice for several centuries with both civic and ecclesiastical records, is an invaluable source for the early appearance of a wide range of English surnames.

Several of these names were coined in connection with occupations.

These include Baker and Smith, while Cooks, Chamberlains, Constables and Porters were to be found carrying out duties in large medieval households.

The church's influence can be found in names such as Bishop, Friar and Monk while the popular name of Bennett derives from the late fifth to mid-sixth century Saint Benedict, founder of the Benedictine order of monks.

The early medical profession is represented by Barber, while businessmen produced names that include Merchant and Sellers.

Down at the village watermill, the names that cropped up included Millar/Miller, Walker and Fuller, while other self-explanatory trades included Cooper, Tailor, Mason and Wright.

Even the scenery was utilised as in Moor, Hill, Wood and Forrest – while the hunt and the chase supplied names that include Hunter, Falconer, Fowler and Fox.

Colours are also a source of popular surnames, as in Black, Brown, Gray/Grey, Green and White, and would have denoted the colour of the clothing the person habitually wore or, apart from the obvious exception of 'Green', one's hair colouring or even complexion.

The surname Red developed into Reid, while

Blue was rare and no-one wanted to be associated with yellow.

Rather self-important individuals took surnames that include Goodman and Wiseman, while physical attributes crept into surnames such as Small and Little.

Many families proudly boast the heraldic device known as a Coat of Arms, as featured on our front cover.

The central motif of the Coat of Arms would originally have been what was sometimes borne on the shield of a warrior to distinguish himself from others on the battlefield.

Not featured on the Coat of Arms, but highlighted on page three, are the family motto and related crest – with the latter frequently different from the central motif.

Adding further variety to the rich cultural heritage that is represented by surnames is the appearance in recent times in lists of the most common names found throughout the United Kingdom of ones that include Khan, Patel and Singh – names that have proud roots in the vast sub-continent of India.

Echoes of a far distant past can still be found in our surnames and they can be borne with pride in commemoration of our forebears.

Chapter two:

Murder and intrigue

Present in Scotland from about the middle of the twelfth century, bearers of the Melville name played key roles in the frequently turbulent affairs of the kingdom, garnering lands, honours and distinction as they did so.

Of Norman roots, they take their name from Galfridus de (of) Maleville who, in turn, hailed from the barony of Maleville in Normandy.

In the retinue of those knights who were rewarded with lands in England in the wake of the Conquest of 1066, he subsequently settled in Scotland during the reign from 1124 to 1153 of King David I.

The king, who had been an exile for a time in the English royal court, had become enamoured with Norman customs, military and organisational skills and enterprise and, accordingly, held out the lure of settling in Scotland by offering them lands.

It is not known precisely which territory, or its extent, this progenitor of the Melvilles of today was granted, but it is known that in 1160, during the reign of King Malcolm IV they held the lands of

Melville – an Anglicisation of 'Maleville' – in Midlothian.

Although this was their original heartland, the family also became established across the River Forth in Fife and came in time to boast prestigious honours including a lordship and an earldom.

The Melvilles prospered from an early date, with Galfridus de Maleville the first appointee to the powerful post of Justiciary of Scotland, and with Melville Castle, about one mile from Dalkeith, established as their seat.

Originally a tower house, it was demolished in the late eighteenth century and replaced by the three-storey Gothic castellated mansion still known today as Melville Castle and built by the celebrated architect James Playfair.

Having undergone a number of changes in ownership over the centuries, it was bought by the Hay Trust in 1993 and, extensively restored, now operates as a hotel and popular venue for functions including weddings.

Going back to the early fifteenth century, one bearer of the Melville name who met with a particularly gruesome end was John Melville of Glenbervie, Sheriff of the Mearns, Kincardineshire.

A thorn in the flesh to local lairds such as George Berclay, 5th Laird of Mathers who frequently flouted the law, in addition to acting with zeal in performance of his legal duties, Melville was also considered arrogant, and these traits combined to make him hated.

So loathed was he that, in 1421, Berclay and two of his uncles and other lairds embarked on a truly murderous course of action to rid themselves of him.

For many years, Murdoch, Duke of Albany, Melville's immediate superior, had endured complaints about his behaviour and unwittingly gave the green light for his murder by exclaiming in exasperation: *"Sorrow gin (if) that sheriff were sodden (drowned) and supped in broo (broth)"*.

Taking this as a cue for action, Berclay and his accomplices invited the unsuspecting Melville to a great feast in a forest, where a large fire and bubbling cauldron of water had already been prepared.

Seized and stripped, he was thrown into the cauldron and, after being boiled for a lengthy time, the gleeful murderers all enjoyed a spoonful of the resultant 'soup'.

Despite the horrific nature of the crime, these

were particularly cruel and vicious times and Berclay and his accomplices were later pardoned for the deed.

Another bearer of the Melville name to meet with a gruesome end was Sir James Melville of Raith, in Fife, executed for treason for his alleged role in the murder of Cardinal Beaton, Archbishop of St Andrews, and for entering into treasonable communication with Scotland's 'auld enemy' England.

The eldest son of John Melville, laird of Raith, through his marriage to Janet Bonar, a daughter of the neighbouring laird of Rossie, his date of birth is not known but he was possibly aged in his early 'twenties when knighted by King James IV in 1503.

One family tradition is that he accompanied the king to the disastrous battle of Flodden, in Northumberland, in 1513.

If so, he was one of the few survivors of this battle in which 5,000 Scots including the king, an archbishop, two bishops, eleven earls, fifteen barons, and 300 knights were killed.

More than 30 years later, in 1546, he was implicated in the murder of the deeply unpopular Cardinal (David) Beaton, Archbishop of St Andrews, Lord Chancellor and Cardinal Legate in Scotland.

This was during the period of religious

upheaval the Protestant Reformation, and Melville was among 300 noblemen, including William Kirkcaldy of Grange and Norman Leslie, Master of Rothes, whom the cardinal had urged King James V to pursue as heretics.

Passions were roused when, on March 1, 1546, the reformer and preacher George Wishart was executed at St Andrews following a show trial over which Beaton had gleefully presided.

Condemned as a heretic, the early Protestant martyr was hanged from a gibbet and, taken down while still alive, burned at the stake – an added horror being that the cardinal had ordered packets of gunpowder to be sewn into his clothing.

A savage revenge followed just over two months later when Kirkcaldy of Grange and Leslie forced their way into St Andrews Castle and murdered Wishart's persecutor, mutilated his body and hung his corpse from the window of a tower.

Kirkcaldy of Grange and other conspirators was caught and executed, but it was not until more than two years later that Sir James Melville was tried for his alleged part in the conspiracy in addition to charges of 'treasonable correspondence' with parties in England – with whom Scotland was then at war.

Found guilty, he was beheaded in Edinburgh on December 13, 1548 by the grim instrument of execution known as 'The Maiden' and his estates forfeited.

But the forfeiture was rescinded fifteen years later in favour of his widow Helen Napier of Merchiston and children.

His second eldest son Robert Melville, 1st Lord Melville, was a highly influential diplomat and political intriguer during the troubled reign of the ill-fated Mary Queen of Scots.

Born in about 1527, he acted as a diplomat for the queen at the court of Queen Elizabeth and then as an envoy to the court on behalf of a rebel body of Scottish nobles opposed to Mary's marriage to Henry, Lord Darnley.

In the complex political machinations of the time, he returned to Mary's favour and became fully committed to her cause following her enforced abdication in July of 1567 in favour of her son, James VI by the body known as the Confederate Lords.

Captured by the lords at the battle of Carberry Hill in July of 1567, she later escaped imprisonment but, on May 23, 1568, forces loyal to her under the command of the Earl of Argyll were routed at the battle of Langside, near Glasgow, and she was forced to flee into what she then naively thought would be the protection of Queen Elizabeth.

She was instead fated for confinement in a succession of strongholds before her execution on February 8, 1587, in the Great Hall of Fotheringhay Castle, in Northamptonshire.

Following her flight into England, meanwhile, Melville had taken her clothing, jewellery and horses while she was in temporary refuge at Bolton Castle and, with other nobles loyal to her, held Edinburgh Castle on her behalf.

Imprisoned for a time following a lengthy siege of the fortress, proving a wily political intriguer and survivor he was rehabilitated and appointed Treasurer-Depute of the Scottish Exchequer and as a judge.

Also having held the post of Chancellor, he was raised to the peerage as Lord Melville of Monimail, in Fife ten years after King James VI's ascension to the English throne as James I.

Overlooking the harbour at Burntisland, in the Forth, his imposing residence Rossend Castle fell into disrepair over the centuries but was restored in 1975 by a local architects' practice and now serves as its office – while one of its painted ceilings, bearing his initials 'RM' is held by the National Museum of Scotland.

Monimail, meanwhile, from which he took the name of his lordship, was the estate near Collessie, in Fife, that came into the family's possession in about 1592.

With a fine touch of irony, bearing in mind his ancestor Sir John Melville of Raith's alleged role in the murder of Cardinal Beaton, The Palace of Monimail, also known as Monimail Tower, had once been a residence of archbishops of St Andrews – including the cardinal.

Overseen by the Monimail Tower Preservation Trust, the tower was painstakingly restored to its former glory throughout the 1990s and early 2000s using historically authentic materials and is classed as a category A listed building.

Chapter three:

Poetry and plots

Not only a diplomat, in common with his older brother Robert Melville, 1st Lord Melville, but also a noted memoirist, James Melville, known as Sir James Melville of Halhill, near Collessie, was born in 1535.

Again in common with his brother he was in service for a time to Mary Queen of Scots, during her sojourn in France, and also carried out a number of diplomatic missions on behalf of the French king Henry II.

Knighted by King James VI in 1590, he is recognised today as a valuable source for the history of his times through his *Memoirs of my own Life*.

He died in 1617, but the manuscript of his memoirs was not discovered until 1663 and published twenty years later by his grandson George Scott.

Through his marriage to Christina Boswell, he had one son and two daughters – one of whom, Elizabeth Melville, Lady Culross, is recognised as the earliest known Scottish woman writer to see her work in print in her lifetime.

Married to John Colville, 3rd Baron of Culross, she was a bitter opponent of the ecclesiastical policies of King Charles I, who sought to impose uniform religious practices between the Church of England and the proudly independent Scottish Kirk.

Her religious convictions and opposition to what she perceived as the tyranny of kings is expounded in her poem *Ane Godlie Dreame – A Godly Dream* – first published in 1603.

She died in 1640 and it was not until nearly 350 years later, in 1988, that she gained true literary recognition.

This was through inclusion in the Australian writer and feminist Germaine Greer's *Kissing the Rod: An Anthology of 17th-Century Women's Verse*, followed in 1991 by *An Anthology of Scottish Women's Verse*, edited by the Scots-Canadian Catherine Kerrigan.

On June 21, 2014 an inscribed flagstone to Elizabeth Melville was unveiled by Germaine Greer in Makars' (Poets') Court, in the Lawnmarket, Edinburgh, the event forming part of a special 'Elizabeth Melville Day'.

Taken from *Ane Godlie Dreame* and in the original Old Scots, the inscription on the flagstone reads:

Though tyrants threat, though Lyons rage and rore
Defy them all, and feare not to win out

One of her paternal uncles was George Melville, 2nd Lord Melville and 1st Earl of Melville, the statesman born in 1636 and who, along with his son David Leslie-Melville, 3rd Earl of Leven, was accused of complicity in a plot to assassinate King Charles II and his brother and heir to the throne the future James II.

As members of the Whig – as opposed to Tory – political faction, they had plotted along with others to clear the way for the succession to the throne of the Protestant William of Orange.

Known as the Rye House Plot, the plan had been to ambush and kill the king and his brother on April 1, 1683, as they were expected to return to London from a horse-racing meet at Newmarket.

But the races were cancelled after a fire broke out, and the royal pair returned early to London – thereby unwittingly aborting the planned attempt on their lives.

But news of the plot nevertheless leaked and Melville and his son fled into exile to the court of William of Orange.

Following the 'Glorious Revolution' of 1688 that saw the Dutchman ascend the British throne as King William III, the Melville father and son were rewarded with titles and honours.

George Melville was appointed Secretary of State for Scotland and, in 1690, created Earl Melville, along with other titles.

He died in 1707 while his son David Leslie-Melville, born in 1660, was appointed a Privy Councillor of Scotland in 1689 and, before his death in 1728, Commander-in-Chief, Scotland – while the home today of his descendants the earls of Leven and Melville is Glenferness House, at Nairn, Inverness-shire.

It was George Melville, 1st Earl of Melville, who had Melville House, adjacent to the Palace of Monimail, built for him in 1697 by the architect James Smith.

With the house having undergone many changes of ownership and use over the centuries, including as a billet for Polish soldiers during the Second World War and a school, it is now a category A listed building and its grounds included on the Inventory of Gardens and Designated Landscapes in Scotland.

In the laboratory, Thomas Melville was the scientist and astronomer born in 1726 at Monimail, the son of the local minister.

Studying under Alexander Wilson, the first professor of astronomy at Glasgow University, in 1749 the pair made the first recorded use of kites in meteorology – using them to measure air temperature at various levels.

As a pioneer in the field of spectroscopy, in his famous lecture Observations on light and colours, delivered in 1752, he described what is recognised as having been the first 'flame test'.

This was when he used a prism to observe a flame coloured by various salts – with a yellow line always seen in the same place in the spectrum.

Also the first to propose that light rays of different colours travel at different speeds, he died in 1753.

At one time the holder of the largest private botanical collection in Britain, James Cosmo Melvill was the botanist and malacologist – someone who studies species that have shells – born in 1845 in Hampstead, London.

A grandson of Sir James Cosmo Melvill, a colonial administrator in India, he entered a cotton merchant business in Lancashire owned by an uncle and became wealthy enough to indulge his passion for botany and malacology.

This interest was aroused at an early age – collecting shells from when he was aged eight and eventually coming to own a collection of 25,500 species of mollusc from all over the world.

His plant collection, kept in a purpose-made building in his garden at his residence Meole Hall, at Meole Brace, Shrewsbury, was said to amount to three-quarters of then known plants in the world, particularly ferns and grasses.

Much of this was later given to institutions including Manchester University, while it now forms part of the collection of the National Botanic Garden of Wales.

A Fellow of the Linnean Society and the Zoological Society of London, he died in 1929.

Yet another botanist was Ronald Melville, a pioneer of research into the medical qualities of rosehips.

Born in Bristol in 1903 and based at the Royal Botanic Gardens Kew, during the Second World War his research into rosehips identified them as an important source of vitamin C – his studies being prompted by an epidemic of scurvy among children because of the much reduced wartime import of fresh fruit.

The Common Dog Rose Rosa canina, he found, held the highest concentration of the precious vitamin.

Also the compiler of the world's first *Red Data Book*, first published in 1970 and listing all known threatened plants and a Fellow of the Linnean Society, he died in 1985 while the tree *Acacia melvillei* is named in his honour.

Chapter four:

On the world stage

Despite failing to achieve due literary recognition in his lifetime, Herman Melville is nevertheless recognised today as the author of one of the great American novels.

Short story writer, novelist and poet of the American Renaissance period of literature, he was born in 1819 in New York City of Scottish and Dutch descent.

The third of three children, through his father the prosperous merchant Allan Melville, he was the great-great-grandson of the Rev Thomas Melville, a minister at Scoonie, in Fife, who died in 1769.

Intriguingly, Melville believed that the minister, in turn, was a descendant of the Protestant reformer Andrew Melville, born at Baldovie, Angus in 1545.

Also noted for the implementation of radical reforms in education at both St Andrews and Glasgow universities, the reformer suffered for the passionate advocacy of his faith by being imprisoned in the

Tower of London between 1607 and 1611 and then banishment to France before his death in 1622.

So obsessed was Allan Melville with his ancestry that he is understood to have visited Scotland on a number of occasions to delve into his roots.

Whether or not this interest was passed to his son Herman Melville is not known, but what is certain is that following his death in 1832 and despite his supposed wealth, his young family was left in a perilous financial state.

Aged 20, and in desperate need of work, Melville took to sea aboard a merchant ship and later a whaler – this experience proving inspirational for his first novel *Typee*, published in 1846 and followed a year later by *Omoo*.

But it was the 1851 classic *Moby Dick* that set him on the path to lasting literary renown.

A tale of whaling in the 1840s, it follows

the unhappy crew of the vessel *Pequod* that sails from Nantucket, Massachusetts, and their captain, Ahab, who is single-mindedly obsessed with the pursuit of the great white shark Moby Dick that took his leg in a previous expedition.

Having taken Melville nearly eighteen months to write, it failed to capture critical acclaim in his lifetime, and it was not until the centennial of his birth in 1919, nearly seventy years after it was first published, that *Moby Dick* received the recognition it deserves.

Regarded as one of the great American novels, it has been the subject of films including the 1956 film of the name with the actor Gregory Peck as Captain Ahab, and a 2011 television mini-series with William Hurt in the role.

Author of a number of other short stories, novels and poetry, he died in 1891, while his unfinished novel *Billy Budd* was published posthumously in 1924.

In 1984, as part of its Literary Arts Series of stamps, the U.S. Postal Service issued a commemorative stamp in his honour – the first place of issue aptly being the Whaling Museum in New Bedford, Massachusetts.

In contemporary literature and also on the stage, **Pauline Melville** is the award-winning short story writer, novelist and actress born in 1948 in Guyana.

Of proud mixed heritage – her mother was English and father of part South American Indian, African and Scottish descent, her big screen credits include the 1986 *Mona Lisa* and, from 1980, *The Long Good Friday*.

As a writer, her collection of short stories *Shape-Shifter*, published in 1990, was the recipient of a number of awards including the PEN/Macmillan Silver Pen Award and a Commonwealth Writers' Prize for Best First Book – while many of the stories deal with post-colonial life in the Caribbean.

Her first novel, meanwhile, the 1997 *The Ventriloquist's Tale*, was winner of the Guyana Prize for Literature and the Whitbread First Novel Award.

Covering genres including Gothic and Victorian mysteries and crime, **Jennie Melville** was a pen-name of the British writer Gwendoline Butler, nee Williams.

Born in South London in 1922, writing as Gwendoline Butler she was the author of the *Inspector John Coffin* series of novels, while as Jennie

Melville she wrote the equally popular *Detective Charmian Daniels* collection that includes the 1962 *Come Home and Be Killed*, the 1988 *Windsor Red* and, from 2001, *Loving Murder*.

Credited with having invented the 'women's police procedural' genre of crime novels, she died in 2013.

On screen, Esme Grace Mount-Melville, born in 1918 in Norwood, South Australia, was the stage, television and film actress better known as **Esme Melville**.

With television credits including the soap *Neighbours*, she was posthumously nominated a year after her death in 2006 in the Australian Film Institute Awards for Best Actress for her role in the film *Romulus, My Father*.

Back on British shores, **Alan Melville** was the multi-talented broadcaster, actor, writer, playwright and producer recognised as one of the nation's first television stars.

Born William Melville Caverhill in 1910 in Berwick-upon-Tweed, Northumberland, it was while working in his family timber business that he also found time to write stories for BBC Radio's *Children's Hour*.

Invited to read the stories himself on air, he also became a full-time BBC scriptwriter in 1936 while, as one of its news correspondents during the Second World War he sent back reports from the D-Day landings on the beaches of Normandy in 1944.

A playwright, his 1949 *Castle in the Air* was adapted for film, as was his 1955 *Full Circle*, while television stardom came through his participation as a panellist on *What's My Line?* and, running from 1957 to 1958, his own show *A to Z*.

He died in 1983 while *Merely Melville*, another of his television shows, is also the title of his autobiography.

Born Jean-Pierre Grumbach in Paris in 1917, **Jean-Pierre Melville** was the influential filmmaker who adopted 'Melville' as a pseudonym during the Second World War as a member of the French Resistance in tribute to his favourite author Herman Melville.

Recognised as the 'spiritual father' of the French New Wave of cinema, with films including the 1962 *Le Doulos* and the 1970 *Le Cercle Rouge*, he died in 1973, while he has influenced the work of other filmmakers including Quentin Tarantino.

In a much different form of entertainment,

Johnny Melville is the Scottish clown, mime artist and actor born in 1948 in Leith.

Credited with having revolutionised the art of the clown and the mime artist, his career began in 1972 in the British theatre scene while he later toured world-wide as a solo performer including at the *Just for Laughs* festival in Montreal, Canada.

As an actor, he was the winner of the 2001 Best Actor Award at the Brooklyn Film Festival for his role in *No Man's Land*, while he has also featured in a number of music videos.

Now married and resident in Denmark, he is the father of the Danish actor and musician **Cyron Bjørn Melville**.

Born in 1984, his first film credit as a child actor was in the 1994 *The Beast Within*, while he later starred in the role of Oliver Schandorff in the television drama series *The Killing*.

Bearers of the Melville name have also excelled in the highly competitive world of sport.

On the football pitch, **Andy Melville**, born in Swansea in 1968, is the former player with teams including Swansea City, Oxford United and Nottingham Forest who won 65 caps playing for his nation between 1989 and 2004.

In rugby union, **Nigel Melville**, born in Leeds in 1961, is the former scrum half and England captain who has held posts including director of professional rugby for Rugby Football Union.

One particularly inventive bearer of the Melville name was **David Melville**, credited as an early pioneer of gas lighting.

Born in 1773 in Newport, Rhode Island, in 1806 he lit up all twenty rooms in his house on Pelham Street by hydrogenous gas he made on the premises by burning coal and wood.

Taking the technique further and to the amazement and delight of his neighbours, he then lit up Pelham Street by means of a large lantern – six years before the first gas lighting appeared in Pall Mall, London.

Melville was granted the first American gas light patent in March of 1810 and, having refined it, a further one three years later.

His invention, however, was some way ahead of its practical application on much larger scales, and it was not until three years before his death in 1856 that a regular gas lighting service was established in Newport – where it had all began fifty years earlier.